Fix the Credit File™

The Ultimate Credit Guide | Build the Future

By Dr. Lisa Hoover

DISCLAIMER AND/OR LEGAL NOTICES:

Dedication

To the ones rebuilding quietly... and those ready to reclaim control.

This guide was born from years of walking beside clients—first as a coach helping entrepreneurs repair personal credit so they could access business funding, and later, as a real estate advisor guiding future homeowners toward financial readiness. But underneath both lanes has always been one constant: the belief that credit isn't just a number. It's a barrier —or a bridge.

I created this guide because people from both my worlds kept asking for the same thing: a clear, honest, and practical path forward. This book is my answer.
It's rooted in education because that's how I serve—and how my mother taught me to lead. *She believed education was the umbrella that should cover every generation, and that belief shapes everything I do.*

To my family—my husband, my children, and my granddaughter **Peanut**—thank you. You remind me daily why this matters.

To my parents, who believed the next generation should always do better than the last: I'm walking that legacy forward.
Let's make sure our traditions come with tools.

— Dr. Lisa Hoover

Table of Contents

Table of Contents

PART I

Credit isn't just a number—it's a gatekeeper to the life you want to build. Whether you're chasing homeownership, launching a business, or simply wanting more financial freedom, your credit report is the silent partner in every major move.

My 2 Cents: *Your credit isn't your worth—but it can shape your access. Learn the game, then master it*

What Makes Up Your Credit Score?

- Payment History (35%)
- Credit Utilization (30%)
- Length of Credit History (15%)
- New Credit (10%)
- Credit Mix (10%)

> ## *My 2 Cents:*
> *If you're going to obsess over one number—make it your **utilization**. That alone can swing your score quickly.*

FICO vs. Vantage: What's the Difference?

FICO = The *traditional scoring system* most of us know-historically and widely used by lenders, with a reputation for being the more authoritative lending score.

VantageScore = Widely encountered through *consumer credit-monitoring* tools and historically viewed by many consumers as an educational score that may run higher or lower than the FICO score a lender sees.

My 2 Cents:

Don't panic over differences. Pick one system and track progress consistently

One FICO Score? Not Quite.

It's a family of scoring models.

There are general FICO Scores, along with industry-specific models designed for different types of lending:

- **Base FICO Scores** — general credit-risk assessment
- **FICO Auto Scores** — designed for auto lending
- **FICO Bankcard Scores** — designed for credit-card lending
- **Mortgage lending** — specific models used for. home loans.

And there are different versions and generations of these models.

VantageScore is a separate scoring system, with its own models and versions.

So when someone says, "*My FICO score is 720,*" there's more to the story:

Which FICO model?
Based on which bureau's data?
For what type of credit decision?

My 2 Cents:

And FICO isn't just one score - which is why the score you see may not be the same score a lender uses. Know which score matters before you start celebrating—or panicking.

Yes—be consistent.

But understand this: the system you're being consistent with is changing.

THE RULES ARE CHANGING

New Credit Score Models

What's shifting- and what it means for your file

VANTAGESCORE 4.0

Launched jointly by the three credit bureaus & gov't agency

2026 update
Mortgage scoring system is changing. Classic FICO remains in use, while some approved lenders can now use VantageScore 4.0 for eligible conventional loans

FICO 10T

T is for trended; meaning analyzes your credit behavior over 24+ months, not just a single snapshot

What changes
Your behavior over time now tells a story. Consistent paydown reads differently than a flat balance month after month.

WHAT THE NEW MODELS WILL INCLUDE

- Rent, phone bills, insurance payments now counted
- Trended data- direction of debt over 24+ months
- Moves from 3 scores to 2- trimerge report remains
- Non-medical paid collections no longer affect scores
- Dormant accounts now counted in calculation
- Expanded access for thin or non-traditional files

IMPORTANT CAVEAT

Adoption is still uneven — most lenders are still using classic FICO. Ask your lender directly: "Which scoring model will you use to underwrite my loan?" That one question changes your entire preparation strategy. Until you know which model your lender uses, don't assume any score you're looking at is the one being evaluated. Ask directly.

My 2 Cents:

This is the system catching up to what your file has always been capable of showing. Rent payments, utility consistency, the direction of your debt- these behaviors demonstrate creditworthiness. The models are finally starting to read them. But until adoption is widespread, the file still has to be built the old way. Know both games.

How to Dispute Errors on Your Report

1. **Pull all three reports**
2. **Highlight inaccurate info**
3. **Dispute online or via mail** *(609 Letter)*
4. **Track your disputes monthly**

My 2 Cents:

Don't dispute everything at once. Target the most damaging errors first and be strategic.

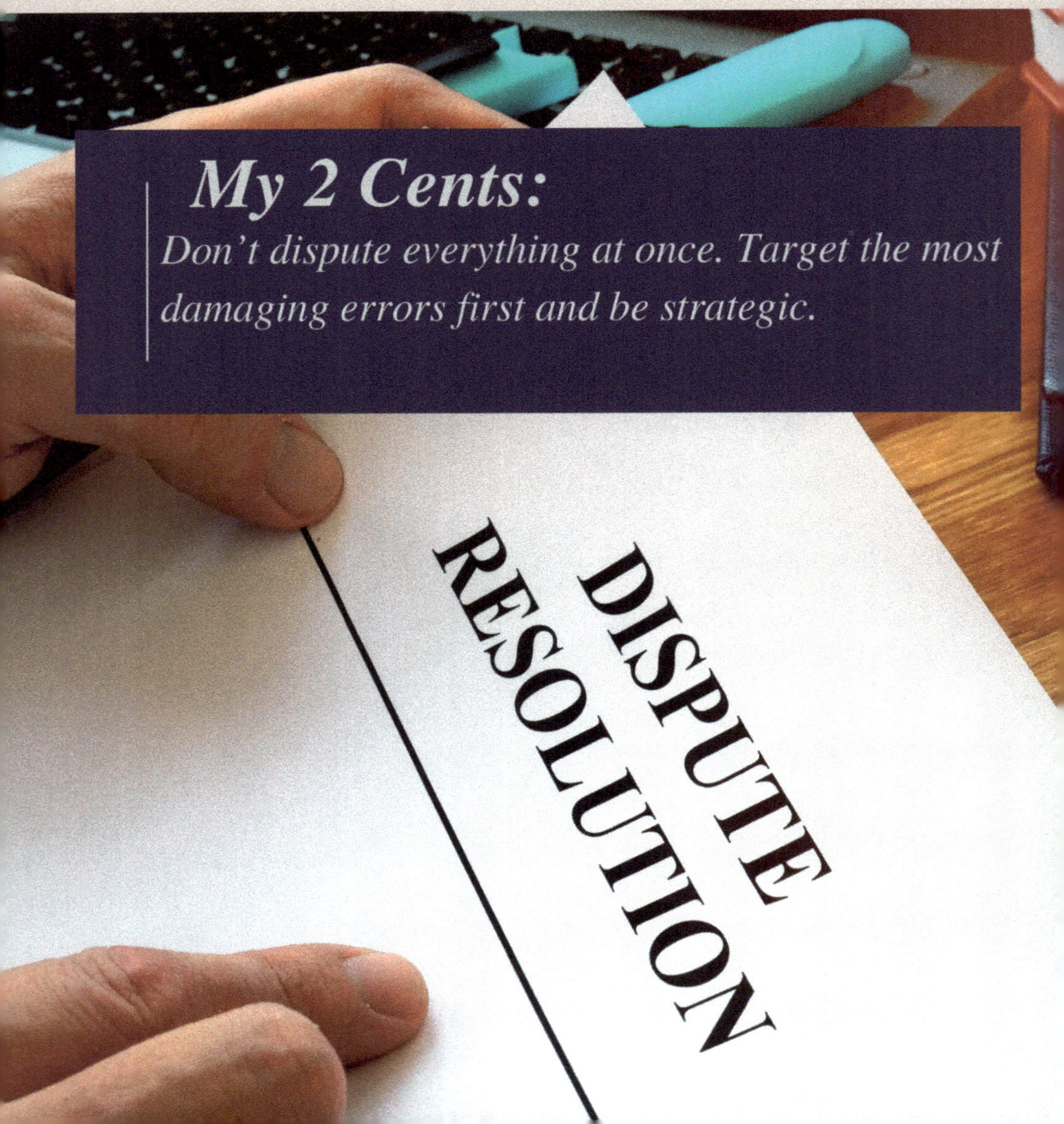

Using Authorized User Strategy Wisely

Pros:

- Piggyback on someone else's good history
- Fast credit age boost

Cons:

- If they miss payments, you're affected
- May not report to all 3 bureaus

My 2 Cents:

Only become an AU on accounts with spotless records and low balances. No exceptions

What Your Credit Can Do (Beyond Buying a Home)

Your credit doesn't just open doors—it expands what you're capable of reaching.

Here are just a few powerful ways it shows up beyond a mortgage:

- Qualifying for a lease
- Lowering insurance premiums
- Starting a business
- Emergency lines of credit
- Building generational wealth

> **My 2 Cents:** *Your credit isn't your worth—but it can shape your access. Learn the game, then master it*

POWER MOVE: BUILDING YOUR CREDIT AS A SOLO FOUNDER

When you're launching solo, consulting, freelancing, or building a one-woman brand; your credit is more than just a number. It's leverage. From vendor approvals to scaling tools, your personal profile opens the door to opportunity.

- **Most solo-preneurs don't qualify for business credit early—so personal credit carries the weight**
- **Use credit cards with reporting benefits and low utilization**
- **Set up business checking and separate expenses now—even if your business is small**

MY 2 CENTS:

Business credit doesn't start with a business—it starts with your personal score. Make sure it's strong enough to carry your vision.

POWER MOVE: STARTING A BUSINESS

With access to credit, dreams of owning a business aren't as far off as they might seem. Use it to fund your start-up, bridge cash flow gaps, or invest in your company's growth.

- **Your personal credit often affects your ability to get a business loan.**
- **Consider net-30 vendors or business credit cards to start separating profiles.**
- **Get an EIN early and register your business with bureaus like Dun & Bradstreet.**

MY 2 CENTS:

Business credit starts with your personal credit. If your foundation isn't strong, your business may not get far. Build it now—before you need it.

POWER MOVE: CREDIT & RENTING

Good credit doesn't just get you into homes you own–it gets you into places you rent. From apartments to single-family leases, landlords often use your credit to screen for risk. Being proactive about your score can mean lower deposits, easier approvals, and more choices.

- **Landlords typically check credit reports before approving leases**
- **Scores under 600 may trigger larger deposits or denials**
- **Late payments and collections are often red flags**
- **You can strengthen your rental profile with consistent payments, low debt, and good references**

MY 2 CENTS:

Your score might not tell your whole story —but it tells a landlord enough to say yes or no. Make sure what they see reflects what you're really about.

POWER MOVE: CREDIT AS EMERGENCY ACCESS

When life happens–unexpected medical bills, car repairs, family emergencies–credit can become your lifeline. Having a solid credit profile means access to fast cash without resorting to predatory loans or draining your savings. It's not about using credit casually–it's about being ready when it matters most.

- Emergency credit options include credit cards, lines of credit, and personal loans
- Good credit means lower interest rates and higher limits when you need them
- Keep at least one low-balance credit card available for emergencies
- Avoid maxing out cards or relying on payday loans

MY 2 CENTS:

Credit is your "break glass in case of emergency" tool. If you wait until disaster strikes to build it, you've already limited your options

POWER MOVE: BUILDING GENERATIONAL WEALTH

Credit isn't just a short-term tool—it's a long game. When used wisely, it can help you build and transfer wealth across generations. From leveraging credit for real estate and investing to simply modeling good habits for your children, credit is part of the legacy you're creating—even if no one handed you one.

- Strong credit allows you to access wealth-building tools like real estate and business funding
- You can co-sign for family members or help them build credit through authorized user status
- Use credit to invest in education, property, or other long-term assets
- Model credit responsibility for the next generation by managing accounts strategically

MY 2 CENTS:

You don't need to come from wealth to build it. Use credit like a key—not just for your goals, but to unlock doors for those coming behind you.

BUILDING + STRATEGIC CREDIT

Improving your credit is like a workout plan—you won't see abs in a week, but you'll see progress if you stay consistent. Use the tools provided (checklist + tracker) and commit to small moves that lead to big shifts.

> **My 2 Cents:** You don't need perfect credit—you need strategic credit. Know the difference.

HOW SCORING ACTUALLY WORKS

The Scorecard

Illustrative ranges only. Actual impact varies by scorecard. The logic is real: every factor has a row, and your file determines where you land.

Payment history

Months since last serious delinquency	
No serious delinquency	75
24+ months ago	55
12-23 months ago	25
0-11 months ago	10

Outstanding debt

Overall utilization on revolving trades	
1-6%	65
7-19%	50
20-49%	45
50-89%	25
90% or more	15

Credit mix

Bankcard trade lines- brand irrelevant		
0 cards		15
1 card		25
2 cards		55
3 cards	sweet spot	60
4+ cards	drops	50

My 2 Cents:

The "30% rule" is a simplification. The real ceiling is 1–6% utilization. 3 bankcards are the sweet spot — not because of brand, but because the scorecard rewards that number. 4+ actually drops. Your file tells the scorecard which row you land in. That's why the file is what matters.

Business CREDIT

Once you've mastered your personal score — here's how to flip that knowledge into ownership

Business Credit: Turning Your Score into Leverage

Before we get fancy with acronyms and scores, let's talk about what this really means.

Your business isn't just paperwork—it's an identity that deserves credit of its own. You've already built credibility with your personal credit story; now it's time to give your business the same respect. This section shows you how to set that foundation, separate the two worlds, and start stacking real leverage- the kind that builds freedom, not just funding.

Understanding the EIN: The Business's Social Security Number

When I'm helping folks set up their business, I always start with this—your business needs *its own Social Security number*. And that's when people usually look at me sideways. But yes, your business gets one too. It's called an Employer Identification Number (EIN), and you apply for it through the IRS. This number gives your business its own identity, just like you have one. For a lot of us—especially those who built small businesses straight from our kitchens or living rooms—no one ever told us about it. We built our dreams out of community, not banks, so we didn't realize this little number could open the door to funding, legitimacy, and opportunity.

Why it matters:

- **It separates your personal identity from your business identity.**
- **It allows your business to pay taxes, open accounts, and establish credibility.**
- **It's the number lenders, suppliers, and vendors use to identify your business on paper.**

The Original Gatekeeper

Before the days of Experian Business or Equifax Business, there was Dun & Bradstreet (D&B)—often the only name that mattered in business credit. For decades, they were the central hub for tracking how businesses paid their bills, handled debt, and managed vendor relationships.

A quick history:
Founded in the 1800s, D&B created a way to measure a company's trustworthiness long before personal FICO scores existed. They assign each registered business a D-U-N-S Number, which acts as your business's ID in the global economy.

Why it matters:

- Many government contracts and corporate suppliers require a D-U-N-S number.
- Your D&B file can show payment patterns, vendor accounts, and credit lines.
- It influences how other companies decide whether to do business with you.
- Creating your *D-U-N-S profile plants a flag that says your business exists,* it's trackable, and it's ready to grow.
- That simple step moves you from hustling in the shadows to operating in the open—where lenders, vendors, and opportunities can actually find you.

> **My 2 Cents:** *Nobody told us D&B was part of the game—but it's been calling plays for decades. Your business credit file isn't just paperwork; it's power. It's how you move from hustling to building, from surviving to scaling.*

Now that we've covered the OG—Dun & Bradstreet—let's talk about the new players on the field

Modern Players: NAV, Experian Business, and Equifax Business

- **NAV (Navigation for Your Numbers)**

NAV serves as a bridge between your personal and business credit worlds. It aggregates information from multiple business bureaus and offers tools to track, monitor, and build your credit profile.

Real Talk: Nav isn't just a credit score website — it's a full business-credit dashboard. It's an online platform (with mobile app) where you can monitor your business credit profiles, your personal ones too, and see how your business data feeds into the major bureaus.

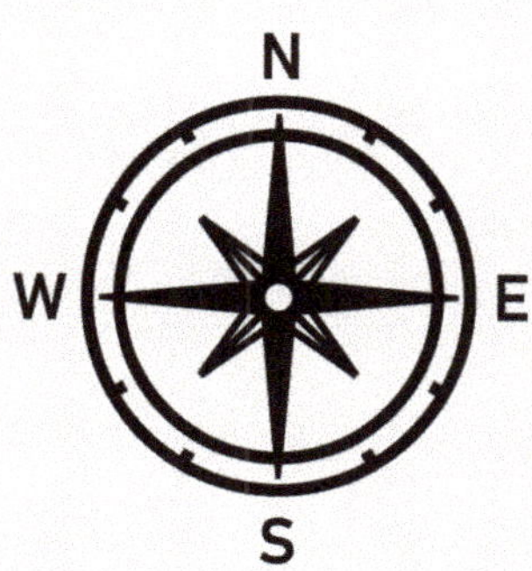

Think of NAV as an online tool and mobile app that serves as your business credit dashboard. It's where you can see:

- **D&B Paydex Score:** A 0–100 scale that measures how promptly your business pays its bills. A score of 80 or higher means you typically pay on time or early.
- **Experian Business Intelliscore:** A 1–100 range used to predict the likelihood of serious delinquency within the next 12 months. Higher scores indicate lower risk.
- **Equifax Business Credit Risk Score**: Evaluates a business's likelihood of late payments or default using a scale typically between 101–992. It combines financial data, trade history, and public records.

NAV doesn't replace these agencies—it helps you see what they see and understand how lenders evaluate your business.

Experian Business & Equifax Business

Call it what it is — capitalism in motion. Experian and Equifax didn't just join business credit; they brought personal data with them. By cross-referencing both worlds, they gained the edge D&B never had — the ability to see you from every angle.They now analyze how companies handle bills, vendor payments, and outstanding debt, linking personal and business profiles in ways that can echo long after you've filed your EIN.

Here's where it gets interesting:

- **These bureaus sometimes link personal and business data — especially for sole proprietors or small LLCs.**
- **In other words, your personal credit story can still echo in your business profile.**
- **They also collect information from trade vendors, business bank accounts, and EIN-linked credit cards.**

My 2 Cents: *They say personal and business credit don't mix—but data always finds a way to cross paths. So build both with intention. Your reputation doesn't stop at your LLC; it travels with your name.*

Real Talk:

Listen, when I first dipped my toes into business credit, I had to laugh to keep from hollering.

How is it that business credit gets this tidy little 0-100 scale, while personal credit has to trek all the way from 0 to 850? Really? It's giving double standard energy.

Here's the kicker: that smaller range doesn't make it easier–it makes every point matter more. Drop ten points in business credit and it hits like losing fifty on your personal side.

The math may look smaller,
but the impact is loud.

Keep your eyes on both stories–the personal and the business–because neither one forgives sloppy math.

Bottom Line: *So yes, it's a 100-point scale, but the game is still rigged if you don't know the rules.*

The Relationship Between Personal and Business Credit

Personal Credit	Business Credit
Measured by FICO & VantageScore	Measured by Paydex, Intelliscore, and Risk Score
Based on SSN	Based on EIN & D-U-N-S #
Reports to Experian, Equifax, TransUnion	Reports to D&B, Experian Business, Equifax Business
Builds with loans, credit cards, and payments	Builds with vendor accounts, trade lines, and business cards
Affects mortgage, auto, and personal loan rates	Affects access to business funding, leases, and contracts

Trade vendors are the suppliers or companies that provide your business with goods or services on credit. Trade lines are the actual credit accounts that those vendor relationships create and report to the business credit bureaus.

Real Talk:

Your business credit isn't a backup plan–it's the blueprint for scale. Build your business profile with the same care you gave your personal one. Because in the eyes of the system, your business becomes an extension of your integrity. And when you nurture that paper trail, you're not just building a company–you're building credibility, opportunity, and access.

Did You Know?

over 70% of minority-owned small businesses operate without a D-U-N-S profile—meaning they're invisible to lenders.

What's hidden behind the numbers? Let's lift the curtain

The same systems that score your personal credit are scoring your business — sometimes before you even realize it.

END RESULT:

Information has become identity, and identity has become currency.

PROTECT YOUR FILE

Buying or Refinancing?

Opt Out First.

When you apply for credit, the bureaus are legally permitted to sell your inquiry data to competing lenders. OptOutPrescreen.com is the official Consumer Credit Reporting Industry website that accepts and processes requests to opt-in or opt-out of firm offers of credit or insurance.

Under the FCRA, Consumer Reporting Companies may include your name on lists used by creditors for "Firm Offers." Opting out stops that.

Protect your privacy

Prevents bureaus from selling your file data to competing creditors

Stop junk mail

End unsolicited creditor offers and mail that follows every inquiry

Stop the calls

Out-of-state lenders can no longer solicit you after your credit is pulled

BEFORE APPLYING

Opt out online at OptOutPrescreen.com — protection lasts 5 years

AFTER CLOSING

Opt out permanently via mail — attempting this before closing may not allow enough time

OFFICIAL RESOURCE

OptOutPrescreen.com

Or call

888-567-8688

Dr. Lisa's Observation

The moment you apply for a mortgage, the bureaus start selling your data. Lenders you never contacted will call you. This isn't a glitch — it's a feature of the system. Opt out before you apply. It's free. It takes five minutes. And it's one of the few moves the system actually allows you to make in your own favor.

Before we go further,
you need to understand
how the score is built —
and why that isn't a contradiction

PART II

Welcome to the backstage of the credit world — where the so-called gatekeepers, whisperers, and powerbrokers run the show. Think of this section as pulling back the velvet curtain to see who's calling the cues behind your credit story. These aren't just faceless data machines; they've each got a personality, a motive, and a history.
Some play it safe, others play favorites — but every one of them plays a part in how opportunity moves.

This is where the illusion ends and the production begins. Because behind every score, report, and "decision" is a system with its own cast of characters — the ones deciding who gets a spotlight and who stays in the dark

Dr. Lisa's Observation:
Power doesn't disappear when systems change — it just rewrites its script.

🎭 The Cast: Meet the Credit Bureaus

TransUnion: The Leasing Whisperer

TransUnion is the quiet middle child of the three bureaus—the one landlords, leasing companies, and auto lenders call first. It has a knack for whispering your rental and payment history into the ears of decision-makers.

Personality: Smooth, calm, and pragmatic. TransUnion doesn't make a scene—it just quietly tells everyone whether you can be trusted with the keys.

Fun Fact: TransUnion has been leaning heavily into rental reporting and tenant screening, which means if you've ever rented an apartment or applied for a car lease, it's probably been talking about you.

> **Dr. Lisa's Observation**: TransUnion might seem low-key, but don't underestimate its influence. It's often the first bureau landlords use, making it a silent gatekeeper for millions of renters and first-time buyers.

Equifax: The Mortgage Gatekeeper

Equifax is the heavyweight in the mortgage game—the one mortgage lenders trust most when making big loan decisions. It's the clipboard-carrying, rule-loving bureaucrat of the group.

Personality: Think of Equifax as the strict head usher—double-checking every ticket at the door. It's meticulous, by-the-book, and obsessed with compliance.

Fun Fact: Many mortgage lenders rely exclusively on Equifax data to determine your eligibility for home loans. It's also the bureau most affected by large-scale data breaches—proof that even gatekeepers need better locks.

> **Dr. Lisa's Observation**: Equifax's reputation as the mortgage gatekeeper isn't just a title—it's a power position. When it comes to homeownership, this bureau can literally make or break access to the dream

Experian: The Overachiever

If Equifax is the rule-follower and TransUnion is the whisperer, then Experian is the flashy overachiever—the one that wants to be seen as both tech-savvy and trustworthy.

Personality: Energetic, image-conscious, and data-hungry. Experian loves innovation—it's the kid that shows up early with color-coded notes and wants extra credit.

Fun Fact: Experian was one of the first bureaus to offer consumer-facing tools like FICO simulators and free score trackers. It's also a key player in both personal and business credit reporting, making it the multitasker of the bunch.

> **Dr. Lisa's Observation**: Experian is the overachiever that keeps reinventing itself. From consumer tools to business analytics, it wants to be the favorite—and for many lenders, it already is.

Information Matters

Once you see the cast, the production doesn't look so intimidating. The goal isn't to fear the system–it's to understand it, so you can work it with confidence.

🕵️‍♀️ The Brokers: The Data Middlemen

If the credit bureaus are the stars, these are the producers—the ones financing and feeding the story.

Behind every score are the unseen brokers: the data gatherers, aggregators, and silent partners who feed the bureaus' reports. They're not household names, but they decide how complete—or incomplete—your credit story looks.

They don't just collect data; they choreograph it. Every transaction, application, and click can pass through their hands before it ever reaches your report.

Dr. Lisa's Observation:
The brokers don't sell stories—they sell access. And who can afford that access shapes the narrative.

LexisNexis: The Legal Powerbroker

Once a direct competitor to Westlaw, LexisNexis carved out its power niche by controlling access to public and legal data. Today, it functions as a silent force in credit reporting, providing background data and verification that influences your credit file.

Personality: Strategic, calculating, and analytical. LexisNexis is the data broker that plays chess while everyone else plays checkers.

Fun Fact: LexisNexis compiles court filings, property records, and even professional licenses—all to create a deep-dive view of your history.

> **Dr. Lisa's Observation**: LexisNexis didn't just collect data—it industrialized it. That's how it became a silent powerbroker in modern credit and risk assessment.

CoreLogic: The Property Sleuth

CoreLogic (and its related platforms) dominates the real estate and property data game. It tracks mortgage applications, rental data, and home valuations.

Personality: Methodical and nosey—the neighborhood watcher of data brokers. If it could talk, it'd start sentences with, "According to our records..."

Fun Fact: CoreLogic provides property-level analytics to lenders, insurers, and even FEMA. If you've ever owned, rented, or insured a property, CoreLogic probably knows about it

> **Dr. Lisa's Observation**: When property data becomes predictive, ownership, insurance, and aid stop being reactive decisions and start becoming pre-filtered outcomes.

Innovis: The Quiet Watcher

Innovis is the underdog of the credit world—the one most people haven't even heard of, but it's been quietly keeping tabs all along. Though smaller than the Big Three, Innovis collects data from lenders, utilities, and cell phone providers.

Personality: Soft-spoken but detail-obsessed. Innovis is like the librarian who remembers every late return.

Fun Fact: Innovis has its own credit reports and even handles fraud alerts—meaning it's small but mighty when it comes to identity verification.

> **Dr. Lisa's Observation**: Innovis shows how influence doesn't always sit with the biggest file — sometimes it lives in background systems that verify identity before a score is questioned.

SageStream: The Comeback Kid

SageStream started as an independent data firm but was eventually folded into LexisNexis Risk Solutions. It built its reputation collecting alternative consumer data like mobile phone accounts and utility payments—information that traditional bureaus used to overlook.

Personality: Ambitious and scrappy—the one that found its lane by seeing what others ignored.

Fun Fact: By focusing on alternative data, SageStream helped shape how modern lenders evaluate people with thin or nontraditional credit files.

> **Dr. Lisa's Observation**: SageStream shows how "*alternative data*" doesn't just expand access — it determines which behaviors are allowed to count when traditional credit falls short.

🎬 Why It Matters

Understanding who's behind the curtain **helps demystify the credit world. These players may shape your financial narrative, but when you know their roles, you stop being a character in their script—you start directing your own.**

Real Talk:
Once you see the cast, the production doesn't look so intimidating. The goal isn't to fear the system—it's to understand it, so you can work it with confidence.

Of course, the old players aren't alone anymore. The digital age brought in new data gatekeepers — quieter, faster, and more complex than anything the original bureaus could've imagined. They're the modern brokers behind the screen. Let's meet them

The curtain rises again – but this time, the players move faster, speak in algorithms, and collect more than whispers. They collect us.

The Bridge

The credit bureaus may have built the original stage, but the data ecosystem rewrote the script. These new players aren't knocking on your door for a payment history — they're already inside your apps, your paychecks, and your clicks. They are the next generation of gatekeepers, the algorithmic brokers shaping how modern credit is scored, tracked, and shared.

Dr. Lisa's Observation: The old system asked if you were trustworthy. The new one assumes you're not until the data says otherwise.

Plaid: The Connector

Plaid is the bridge between your bank accounts and your favorite money apps. It lets apps like Venmo, CashApp, and Robinhood access your transaction history so they can "*verify*" your financial profile.

Personality: Friendly but nosy — the one who wants to "*help*" but always asks for your login first.

Fun Fact: If you've ever linked your bank account to a budgeting app, you've probably used Plaid without knowing it.

> Dr. Lisa's Observation: Plaid helped usher in a new era where data wasn't just about debt or creditworthiness. Your deposits, transfers, purchases, and habits became part of a larger financial story–and stories have value.

The Work Number: The Employer's Whisper Network

Owned by Equifax, The Work Number verifies employment and income information for millions of workers. Employers and lenders use it to confirm stability, often without workers realizing how detailed the data exchange is.

Personality: The HR insider — formal, efficient, and quietly invasive.

Fun Fact: It holds records for over 150 million employees and sells access to that data to banks, landlords, and government agencies.

Real Talk: The Work Number reminds us that even your paycheck has a paper trail — and someone else is reading it.

> Dr. Lisa's Observation: The Work Number gives Equifax a front-row seat to more than credit. With records covering millions of workers, it sits at the intersection of employment, income, and access. That's worth paying attention to because verification has become its own form of power.

Acxiom: The Ad Broker Turned Data Dealer

Acxiom started as a marketing data company but evolved into one of the world's largest data collectors. It compiles profiles on billions of consumers worldwide, connecting marketing, purchasing, and behavioral data.

Personality: The extrovert of the data world — always watching, always networking.

Fun Fact: Acxiom reportedly holds thousands of data points per consumer, influencing not just what ads you see but what lenders think you'll do next.

> Dr. Lisa's Observation: Acxiom didn't start in finance – it started in marketing. But when behavioral data became financial data, the line between 'what you buy' and 'whether you qualify' disappeared.

Envestnet | Yodlee: The Shadow Accountant

Often working behind the scenes of financial tech apps, Envestnet | Yodlee aggregates and analyzes user financial data for banks, lenders, and fintech companies. It's the quiet analyst, turning your swipes into scoreline.

Personality: The data whisperer — analytical, efficient, and rarely seen in the spotlight.

Fun Fact: It provides financial data to over 1,000 institutions and powers insights for fintech tools around the world.

> Dr. Lisa's Observation: Yodlee reminds us that data doesn't always need to be created—it can simply be collected, combined, and interpreted. Sometimes the complete picture is worth more than any single piece.

Early Warning Systems: The Banker's Radar

As a consortium owned by major U.S. banks, Early Warning Systems (EWS) monitors checking and savings account behavior. It flags overdrafts, fraud, and account closures — long before traditional credit bureaus ever see them.

Personality: The security guard of the financial world — protective, suspicious, and always watching the door.

Fun Fact: EWS powers Zelle, which means your peer-to-peer payments are part of a much bigger data story.

> Dr. Lisa's Observation: Credit bureaus aren't the only scorekeepers. Early Warning Systems reminds us that checking accounts, savings accounts, overdrafts, and payment activity can become part of a larger story about risk–and that story may begin long before a mortgage application.

THE WEIGHT BENEATH EVERY CREDIT REPORT

Fade to Credit(s): What It All Means

These are the supporting cast — the digital brokers writing modern financial scripts. They may not assign your score, but they influence how every lender, app, and algorithm interprets your story. In a world where data moves faster than dialogue, understanding their roles changes everything. Because once you see who's behind the curtain, you stop chasing approval — and start directing your own narrative.

Real Talk: Every tap, swipe, and transaction leaves a trail. And just like in Hollywood, the supporting cast can sometimes steal the scene.

What You're About to Read Matters

SPECIAL REPORT » How the Score Story Unfolds

The Score Story Gazette

Uncovering the real story of credit, access, and inequality

SPECIAL REPORT

EXTRA! EXTRA!

SPECIAL REPORT

The Score Story: Receipts & Realities

The Ledger Never Lies

Credit didn't start with a score — it started with a story. Long before the numbers and algorithms, there were ledgers, whispers, and handwritten notes in bank margins deciding who was "good for it." This section pulls out the receipts — the historical ones and the hidden ones — to show how the credit system evolved, who it served, and who it sidelined.

We're stepping into journalist mode now. The who, what, when, where, and why of credit are all here — not the glossy brochure version, but the real story: messy, revealing, and long overdue for review. Think of this section as the investigative issue of your financial newspaper — a blend of archive and exposé.

SPECIAL REPORT

The Score Story: Receipts & Realities

The Early Scripts — From Trust to Tracking

The first form of credit wasn't digital. It was personal. Merchants extended trust based on relationships, reputation, and sometimes race or gender. Your name in a small-town ledger was your score. No algorithm. No appeal. Just judgment written in ink.

Then came modernization — the Industrial Age met bureaucracy. By the early 1900s, companies like Retail Credit Company (which would become Equifax) began compiling personal files on millions of Americans. It wasn't just about whether you paid your bill. These reports tracked where you lived, how often you moved, and even what kind of neighbors you had. The scorecard of your life had begun.

Dr. Lisa's Observation:

The earliest credit reports weren't about money — they were about morality. The system didn't just assess whether you could pay; it judged whether you should be trusted.

Now Consider the Cost.

The Receipts: When Credit Got a Formula

By the 1950s, the business of trust had become too big for gossip. Enter FICO — ***Fair Isaac Company*** — a data-driven attempt to standardize judgment. They promised fairness through math. A formula that could replace bias with logic. But as history shows, when humans write the formulas, the bias doesn't disappear — it just learns to code.

That's where the receipts start piling up: redlining maps that blocked entire Black neighborhoods from loans, "risk models" that coded zip codes as destiny, and generational gaps in access that still echo today.

SPECIAL REPORT

The Score Story: Receipts & Realities

Real Talk:

The credit system didn't accidentally miss us – it was designed without us in mind. For generations, access to financial opportunity wasn't an oversight; it was an exclusion plan written in policy and practice. From redlined maps to denied business loans, the message was clear: who you were–and where you came from–determined what you could build.

But here's the truth they never printed: even if the system wasn't built for us, we've learned how to navigate it, challenge it, and rewrite it. Knowing that truth doesn't just expose injustice–it gives you the blueprint to flip the script

Then & Now:

Fast forward to the present. We've got VantageScores, apps, and instant approvals, but the power dynamic hasn't shifted much. Behind the digital dashboards and friendly interfaces, the same gatekeepers still hold the keys.

The myth is that credit is objective — a clean, mathematical measure of risk. The reality? It's a mirror, and what it reflects isn't just numbers, but the story of inequality coded into our economy. Every data point, from your zip code to your payment history, carries traces of past systems — who got access, who was denied, and who had to build credit in the margins. When we look closer, the reflection shows more than our financial habits; it reveals how history still scores us.

Then & Now (cont'd):

That's the quiet weight beneath every credit report — a story still unfolding. *Algorithms* may have replaced the clerks with ledgers, but the assumptions remain baked into the data. When an algorithm sees a low score, it doesn't ask why; it just reacts. It doesn't see the mother who paid cash because her bank once denied her. It doesn't count twenty years of rent paid on time—because rent was never reported. Modern credit systems measure outcomes, not effort — and in that gap between intention and interpretation, entire communities still pay the price.

The Reality Check – Modern Credit's Mask

Then & Now (cont'd):

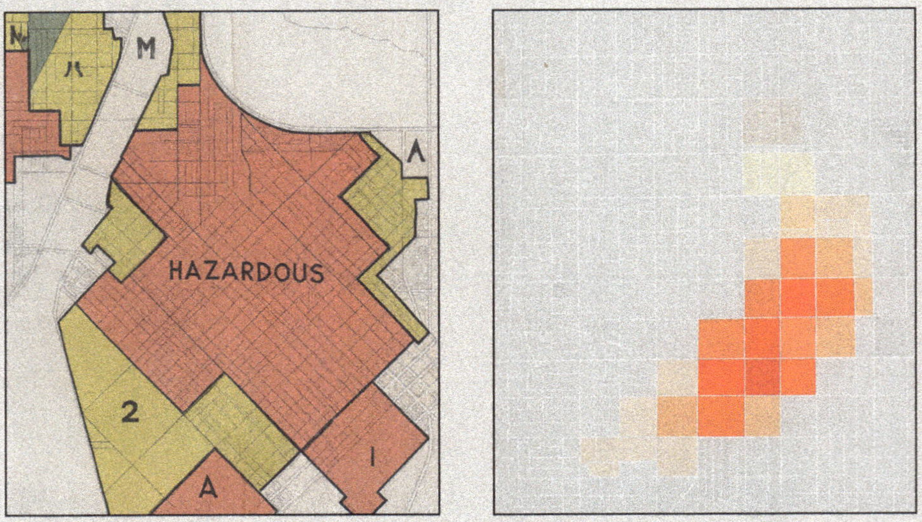

Different Tools, Same Lines.

**REDLINING–
THEN & NOW**

Dr. Lisa's Observation:
Credit scores don't just measure risk. They often measure access — to stable income, homeownership, and generational opportunity..

SPECIAL REPORT

The Reconstruction – What Comes Next

Just like the historical Reconstruction era that followed the Civil War, this moment in credit is a rebuilding phase — a chance to reconstruct the economic framework in a way that recognizes what was broken and intentionally includes those who were left out. The original Reconstruction tried to rebuild a nation after generations of systemic exclusion; today, financial reconstruction means reimagining access and rewriting who gets to participate in wealth-building.

If history shows anything, it's that every system can be rewritten. Credit is evolving again — with new models that include rent, utilities, and alternative data. It's not perfect, but it's progress. The receipts are shifting, and so can the narrative.

FROM RECEIPTS TO RECONSTRUCTION

SPECIAL REPORT

The Reconstruction – What Comes Next

The next chapter of credit doesn't belong to the bureaus. It belongs to those who understand the story well enough to rewrite it.

Receipts Across Time: *The Score's Long Story*

1930s	Maps label communities of color 'hazardous' for investment
1968	Fair Housing Act forbids housing discrimination
1977	Community Reinvestment Act encourages funding in all communities
2025	Digital lending still shows approval gaps for applicants of color

Different Tools, Same Lines.

SPECIAL REPORT

The Reconstruction – What Comes Next

The next chapter of credit doesn't belong to the bureaus. It belongs to those who understand the story well enough to rewrite it.

RECEIPTS IN THE LAW

Know Your Rights

Fair Credit Reporting Act (FCRA)

Protects the accuracy, fairness, and privacy of credit information.

- **Translation:** You have the right to dispute and demand corrections.

Equal Credit Opportunity Act (ECOA)

Prohibits discrimination in credit decisions based on race, gender, or other identity factors.

- **Translation:** Fair access isn't optional—it's federal law.

Fair Housing Act (FHA)

Protects your right to equal access to mortgages and housing credit.

- **Translation:** Your zip code shouldn't decide your future.

PROGRESS OR PATTERN?

Year / Era	The Receipts (What Happened)	The Reality (What's Still True)
1930s	HOLC Redlining Maps created	Loan denials and appraisal bias still mirror old boundaries
1956	FICO founded	Algorithmic scoring still amplifies existing inequality
1968	Fair Housing Act signed	Racial gaps in homeownership persist at near-1968 levels
1970	Fair Credit Reporting Act enacted	Credit reporting errors remain the top FTC complaint
2010	CFPB established	Most credit disputes still favor institutions, not individuals
2025	Fix the Credit File™ movement	Finally reframing credit as education, not exclusion

Real Talk:

When you know how the story started,, you get to decide how it ends

PART III

Introduction:The Gateway to Your Dream Home

Credit is not just a number; it is your golden ticket to homeownership. Whether it is unlocking better loan terms,
qualifying for down payment assistance, or simply making your dream home affordable, Credit plays a **starring role but it is not the star.** This guide is your compass to navigate the credit jungle and emerge ready to buy.

Before we talk steps, let's talk context. Yes, you need to know the acquisition process — but you also need to understand the room: who's reading your file, what they're looking for, and why that changes everything

You'll hear:

- Talk to lenders
- There's no single cutoff

Both statements are true.

But none of that changes the file.

Lenders don't fix files — they read them.

So, if the pattern in the file doesn't work, changing the lender doesn't change the outcome.

"Before we talk about assets, let's stop pretending this is neutral."

Pulling Your Credit File

Not all credit pulls are equal — and how you pull matters as much as what you find.

FOR MONITORING

AnnualCreditReport.com

Free. Official. All three bureaus — Equifax, Experian, and TransUnion.

FOR MORTGAGE READINESS

myFICO.com

Paid (~$40 one-time). Gives you the actual mortgage scoring models lenders use.

Pull strategy

- Pull one bureau at a time — space them out
- Save the reference number from each pull
- That number ties any dispute back to that exact report version — it matters procedurally

What myFICO gives you

- FICO Score 2 (Experian),
- Score 5 (Equifax),
- Score 4 (TransUnion)
- These are the classic mortgage scores used in a traditional tri-merge pull
- Your lender takes the middle score of the three

Important Distinction

Free tools like Credit Karma use VantageScore — useful for monitoring trends but not what your mortgage lender sees. myFICO is worth the cost specifically when you are 60-90 days out from applying. Not as an ongoing tool — as a readiness check.

Dr. Lisa's Observation

Most buyers walk into a lender's office having only seen their Credit Karma score. That number and the lender's number are often not the same — and the gap is always a surprise. Pull your actual mortgage scores before you apply. Know your number before they do.

OVERVIEW : Mindshift

Let's face it: our historical mindset around credit hasn't always been the smartest GPS for navigating today's financial highways. Instead of fearing it or ignoring it, think of your credit report as a part-time job—one that demands a little attention, a few smart strategies, and a knack for problem-solving. The process may not be glamorous, but here's the payoff: mastering it is the key to unlocking the doors of your dream home. The next pages will walk you through a step-by-step guide to make the homebuying process smoother, smarter, and within reach.

Step 01 Know Where You Stand

1. **Pull Your Credit Reports:**
   a. **Get your free reports**
   b. **Make sure to review all three reports —Equifax, Experian, and TransUnion.**
2. **Check Your Score:**
   a. **Use tools like Credit Karma (*for estimates only*)**
   b. **Ask your bank for your actual *FICO* score.**
3. **Spot Errors**
4. **Dispute inaccuracies like outdated debts or accounts you didn't open. This can give your score an instant boost.**

Knowledge is only useful when applied

Step 02 Tackle Debt with Precision

1. **Pay Bills On Time, Every Time:**
   - ***Payment history is 35% of your score. Late payments are like red flags to lenders.***
2. **Target High Credit Card Balances:**
   - ***Aim for a credit utilization ratio below 30% (or 10% if you're ambitious).***
   - ***Example: If your limit is $1,000, keep your balance below $300.***
3. **Don't Close Old Accounts:**
   - ***Keep older accounts open; they lengthen your credit history.***
4. **Avoid Big Purchases:**
   - ***Financing furniture or a car now? It could impact your debt-to-income ratio, which lenders scrutinize.***

Step 03 Build Credit Smartly

1. **Become an Authorized User:**
    - **Ask a trusted friend or family member to add you to their credit card. Then you'll inherit their good payment history.**
2. **Use a Secured Credit Card:**
    - **If your score is low, this is a safe way to build credit. Make small purchases and pay them off monthly.**
3. **Diversify Your Credit Mix:**
    - **A mix of credit cards, loans, and installment credit (like a car loan) shows you can handle various types of debt.**

Step 04 Keep Your Eyes on the Prize

1. **Limit Hard Inquiries:**
   - **Each credit pull for a loan or credit card dings your score slightly. Avoid unnecessary applications*.**
2. **Set Credit Goals:**
   - **Track progress monthly. Tools like *NerdWallet* or *Credit Sesame* can help you visualize your improvements.**
3. **Save for a Down Payment:**
   - **While improving credit, build your savings. Strong credit + a solid down payment= mortgage magic.***

- ***this is not true for mortgage applications***
- *sometimes your downpayment can be smalller than you think**

@lisahooverrealtor

Step 05 Understand Credit's Impact on Home Loans

Here's what a difference a few points can make:

- **580: The minimum for FHA loans, but expect higher interest rates.**
- **620: Opens doors to conventional loans.**
- **740+: You're a lender's dream and eligible for the best rates and terms.**

Mortgage Readiness Reality Check

- **Meet with a Lender Early:**
  - **A lender can review your financial situation and provide a roadmap to mortgage readiness.**

- **Understand Assistance Programs:**
  - **Many programs cater to first-time buyers with lower credit scores or limited savings.**

- **Budget Beyond the Mortgage:**

- **Consider taxes, insurance, and maintenance.**

Mortgage readiness isn't a score.
It's a pattern.

@lisahooverrealtor

Final thoughts

BUILDING CREDIT ISN'T ABOUT PERFECTION. IT'S ABOUT PROGRESS

- **A process to navigate, not a one-time task.**
- **An integral part of achieving long-term goals like buying a home, financial freedom or starting a business**
- **A balancing act between multiple financial and personal priorities.**

Improving credit is like planting a tree. The sooner you start, the sooner you'll reap the rewards. With diligence, knowledge, and a bit of strategy, you can make this the year you unlock the door to your dream home.

Ready to take the next step? Let's make your home-buying dreams a reality!

Visit my website:
www.lh-re.co
@lisahooverrealtor

Just keep
moving forward
@drlisahoover1

APPENDIX.

Resource Guide

Government & Legal Resources

Where Access Meets Action

Category	Description	Notes
Federal Trade Commission (FTC)	Oversees consumer protection laws and credit reporting compliance.	FTC.gov/credit – File complaints about credit bureau violations or identity theft.
Consumer Financial Protection Bureau (CFPB)	Handles consumer credit disputes, lender complaints, and financial education.	ConsumerFinance.gov – Submit credit bureau or lender complaints; review educational tools.
AnnualCreditReport.com	Federally authorized source for your free annual credit reports from all three bureaus.	Access reports directly; check for errors and dispute inaccuracies.
Equal Credit Opportunity Act (ECOA)	Protects consumers from discrimination in lending.	Learn your rights when denied credit or facing unfair terms.
Fair Credit Reporting Act (FCRA)	Governs accuracy and privacy in credit reporting.	Know when to dispute, how long items can stay on your report, and your rights to correction.

Educational Tools

Resource	Description	Notes
FICO® Score Education Center	Free tutorials on understanding your credit score and factors that influence it.	MyFICO.com/Credit-Education – Learn how payment history, balances, and new credit impact your score.
Experian Resource Library	Articles, videos, and simulators for improving credit.	Experian.com/education – Use tools to explore credit scenarios, not as personal financial advice.
Equifax Learning Hub	Resource center for credit-building, fraud protection, and small business credit insights.	Equifax.com/personal/education – Helpful for understanding bureau data structure.
Credit Karma Education	Explains consumer finance topics in plain language.	Great for beginners — but remember, their "score" isn't your FICO® score.

Small Business & Entrepreneur Credit Tools

Resource	Description	Notes
Dun & Bradstreet Small Business Portal	Access D-U-N-S® numbers, business credit reports, and learning tools.	DNB.com – Check if your business is listed and request a D-U-N-S® profile.
NAV Business Credit Builder	Monitors business credit scores and links with multiple bureaus.	Nav.com – Track business credit, but confirm data accuracy directly with bureaus.
SBA Learning Center	Offers free courses on financing, credit readiness, and business planning.	SBA.gov/learning-center – Especially useful for women and minority-owned startups.

Identity Protection & Fraud Prevention

Resource	Description	Notes
IdentityTheft.gov	Central government portal for identity theft recovery and prevention.	Step-by-step plans for reporting stolen information.
OptOutPrescreen.com	Official site to opt out of pre-approved credit offers.	Reduces junk mail and minimizes exposure of personal data.
HaveIBeenPwned.com	Checks if your personal or business email was exposed in a data breach.	Use for awareness only — don’t input passwords.

Access is only Power when paired with Awareness. These resources aren't endorsements- they're navigation tools. When you know where to go, you Stop reacting and start directing.

DEDICATED

CREDIT CLARITY NOTES

DEDICATED

CREDIT CLARITY NOTES

DEDICATED

CREDIT CLARITY NOTES

Fix the Credit File™

Education + Elevation.
No Fog.

You've seen behind the system- now let's fix it. Join Fix the Credit File™ and take your credit journey further.

www.ingramcontent.com/pod-product-compliance
Lightning Source LLC
LaVergne TN
LVHW050937210926
848482LV00013B/653
* 9 7 9 8 9 9 9 3 9 0 3 3 2 *